IN FORBIDDEN LANGUAGE

IN FORBIDDEN LANGUAGE

poetry by

Dah

Stillpoint Publishing / Stillpoint Press
Spokane, Washington

Cover Photo and Design: Dah

Back Cover Design: Scott Fitzgerald

Page Layout and Design: Dah and Eve Hogard

Stillpoint Press Logo: V. Kipp Ashford

Final File Prep: Scott Fitzgerald

Cataloging Data

Dah, 1950 –

In Forbidden Language : poems / by Dah. – 1st ed.

ISBN 978-0-9828747-0-7

Printed in the United States of America.

Stillpoint Publishing / Stillpoint Press

Eve Hogard, Publisher

Spokane, WA U.S.A.

www.mystillpoint.net

for Heike and Annika

If you find yourself being too careful
then you may not find yourself at all.

Dah

Introduction

Others have praised Dah's poetry long and passionately. My life's work is about getting these themes into the world as articulately as possible: That all life is sacred, and that we are the architects of our universe, each a microcosm within a macrocosm full of mysteries, challenges, and triumphs. I approached Dah to publish this work because I believe it exemplifies these themes, takes them to new levels, and is simply a joy to read. I had to have his work in my library. On that note, here's a little something about Dah.

٭,٭,٭,٭

I love this story: When Dah was 11, he upset his neighborhood parish Catholic Church for refusing to call the priest Father, citing some careful research he'd done to explain his position. The priest told him he was possessed by the devil, and had no right to interpret the word of *God*. Dah left Catholicism, and has been willfully interpreting the words of *God* ever since.

Some years later, Dah was drafted into the U.S. Army—during the Vietnam era. Within a couple of years, spiritual depletion led to exploration of yoga, meditation, and similar paths of inquiry. First-hand experience with the power of existence and the responsibility of selfhood (heightened by the interactions within that era of the early 1970s) encouraged a dedicated lifetime of passionate soul searching.

Absolutely spiritual in its transcendental approach, this work is at once a rejection of dogma and a call to connectedness. Following the heritage of *Walden*'s whisper of meditative appreciation and rugged individuality, these pieces celebrate the natural world around us, and call us to pay attention.

٭,٭,٭,٭

I also love this story: In 2003, Dah did not think of himself as a writer, though he wrote passionately and often. As an artist, his expression at that time was primarily photography. Swami Sita approached Dah at a yoga teacher training in Grass Valley, California, and with very little previous contact she asked if she could do a reading for him. She told him this: Writing is your gift.

So, with pleasure, I present to you this first book-form package of Dah's many gifts. *In Forbidden Language* is a collection gathered for you, to open your mind and your heart with cathartic language and thought-provoking juxtapositions. Revel in the celebratory and unapologetic tone, and be inspired to appreciate the sensual wonders of being alive. *In Forbidden Language* is a work of love and a *Song of Songs* for the modern age. It is my privilege to help bring this beautiful collection of writings into the world. I hope you find it inspiring and enjoyable.

And when you get a chance, look him up on OriginalPoetry.com. As of this writing in 2010, you're sure to find a community of poets in discussion on these themes.

Namaste.

Eve Hogard
October, 2010
Vinegar Flats
Spokane, Washington

FORMATTING NOTE: Pieces in this book placed at the bottom of the page are journal entries—lyrical, not quite poetry, with no titles and not included in the Table of Contents—like secret bonus material in this seasonal opera of life-affirming work. I hope you enjoy these real-time snippets from a beautiful mind. —EH

Author's Statement

Each person has his or her own truth, holding to it like an essential loving companion for the heart and soul. It makes no difference if we agree or disagree with one another as long as we are true to ourselves, to our beliefs, visions, and ideas, without fear, contradiction, or domination over others.

We live in reality, yet most of our realities are constructed from, or form, different realities: My reality is not yours, yours is not mine: What I write about is my life; my existence; my philosophy to live by. I do not ask that anybody follow, accept, or agree with my ideas, and if what I write about happens to align with your heart and soul then a part of our destiny has been reached by the miraculous order of spiritual satisfaction.

Mind is bigger, more powerful, more magical, than most of us understand, or are told, it to be. Love, freedom, peace, and light must exist in our thoughts before manifesting into reality, into our lives. Trust and believe in yourself, for the ultimate truth lies within:

To see the full expression

or the blooming reality

of a tightly closed rosebud,

the bud must believe

in itself from within

to express its full,

glorious freedom.

Acknowledgments

These poems have received the following awards or have appeared in the following publications:

The Artists Embassy International Poetry Prize: "A Shawl Of Indigo Aura"

The International Library of Poetry Publishing Award: "Through The Channels"

Original Poetry Anthology 2009: "Then The Tumblers Rust"

Original Poetry Anthology 2010: "If I Ask The Dead For Memories"

Many blessings to Eve Hogard of Stillpoint Press for finding my Web page, reading my poems, contacting me, and publishing me. I could not have had a more spiritual being guiding me through my first book publication. *Eve, you have made this experience a memorable one!*

Special thanks to these poets, teachers, and critics for contributing to the back-cover comments: Award-Winning Poet Linda Bratcher Wlodyka (www.originalpoetry.com/poet/ginga); Poet, Novelist, and Literary Critic Oren O. Cousins, B.A. (www.originalpoetry .com/poet/cousinsoren); A poet friend//RH Peat (www.originalpoetry .com/poet/RHPeat); Award-Winning Poet Mary Anne Anderson (www.originalpoetry.com/poet/aria). Please, visit their Web pages and read their poems.

An endless thanks to my wife Heike and to my daughter Annika for their ideas and suggestions for the cover design, and again to Heike for choosing the cover photograph, and again to Annika for hand texturing the photograph.

A very special thanks to my long-time friend of twenty-seven years, the writer Afaf Kanafani, whose contentment, love, and inner harmony has always been the perfect spiritual inspiration and creative influence—she is very special to me, and at 92, a blazing flame. Visit her website.

I give thanks to writer Michael Grotsky who, for several years, continually pushed my imagination and constantly presented me with creative writing challenges, and for editing some of my many poems and unpublished manuscripts.

To poet Marianne Robinson for inviting me and encouraging me to read at the Berkeley Unitarian Hall open-mike nights in which she was the Master of Ceremonies for ten years.

I stand and applaud my circle of friends from OriginalPoetry.com who, for the past one-and-a-half years, have given superb intellectual critiques, suggestions, and support on many of the poems appearing in this book.

Last but not least, I am forever grateful to the past and present poets who have inspired my thoughts and my writing, and who have influenced my motivation to remove the walls and search for my self.

Thank you everybody for all of your contributions to this book that has been in the making for the past ten years, to a book that has been through the rejection process many times, and that has passed through a few metamorphoses—from a dusty gray caterpillar to a multi-colored butterfly.

Quotes and Credits

Where light formed for us before breath—Ukrainian Poet Paul Celan

Lightning returns *intense and swift*—French Poet Arthur Rimbaud

To the mysterious scents that shake my soul—French Poet Arthur Rimbaud

To be sane with love—French Poet Arthur Rimbaud

Thoughts are vital active energy—American Writer Charles Haanel

All things come from within—American Writer Charles Haanel

To encircle the primal mother—Portuguese Poet Fernando Pessoa

All life, God, change it or end it—inspired by a line from Portuguese Poet Fernando Pessoa

If we were to stretch our minds and touch another universe, our consciousness would duplicate our souls—inspired by a poem from Portuguese Poet Fernando Pessoa

The Captain's Verses—poetry book title of Chilean Poet Pablo Neruda

I envy (in a manner of speaking)…—French writer and founder of Surrealism André Breton, from his novel, *Nadja.*

Table Of Contents

AUTUMN

I wander through the midst of colorful falling things, like leaves and insects, with light follies of rain: feathery showers under the precipitous presence of ample, gray clouds.

To Fill This Page

To fill this page
I must empty my doubt,
holding fast to the joy
of ambition.

A meditation: Creation is a revelation
expanding in silence.
What brought us to earth?
What binds us to the promise of language?

With words liberating this poem,
each phrase is an abundance of precise sounds.
I admire the power of verbs, and
make a wish: *to sail upon the silence of light.*

Light streams into our veins
like cosmic opium or
like lovers who live
for being inside of each other.

I demand too much from the universe, and
speaking of this is like an iron trap suffering from rust.
I write this down so as not to fill my feelings
with emptiness. Soul:

My bliss, my enthusiast
—I must speak of this
to understand these burning lines.

As I Exist

As I exist
across the universe,
I seek light and
must not enter dark holes.

With gratitude
I face the sun,
and rely on the power
of burning desire.

I imagine *God*
drunk on arrogance
—his soul
has no cloud-clothes on—

he is weightless
and composed of haze or smog
and human sacrifice.
Sometimes in the sky

I see all of humanity's prayers
asking for forgiveness:
Whose soul is without sin?

How We Live On Earth

How we live on earth: It would be better
if we were flocks of doves or creatures living in the seas.

Behind our memories we've put certain things away:
*Our primal origin, primal sex, primal slithering (from before
we grew legs), primal gills, God's absence, primal scales*

—behind our memories we've put these things away,
no longer listening to the voice of falling snow
(human clumsiness forbids this).

Love has become a crippled master.
Loneliness cheats at solitaire.
Hate beats on drums of human skin.
Light hardens inside closed hearts.

Forgetting is a sunken ship with dead memories
—we have forgotten our origins: *the seaweed we used to eat,
the taste of sea salt in our blood, the voices of whales,
a sea star's stillness,*

*the absolute bottom of the ocean,
the evolution of sea sponges into humans.*
Behind our memories we've put these things away.

We Are Not Finished

We are not finished
in knowledge, nor in wisdom,
nor in love. Chained to
human clumsiness, we
make ourselves more clumsy

with our audacious arrogance,
with our wandering ignorance,
with our lack of enthusiasm
for love-absolute.

The mind's
demanding motion
gathers no silence
within its inexhaustible rumors:

A chaotic nervousness fingers its way
into our dreams—nightmares!
—to the point of perfect
spiritual depletion.

I speak of this
only to remind myself
of religion's deception:

in leaving the spiritually weak faithfully helpless
—for schooling them in spiritual fantasies,
and for leading them into holy deceptions.

Nothing is sacred
and everything is.

Creation.

Is not.

Sacred. Creation:

a multitude of stars exploding.

I Promise To Imagine

I promise to imagine
and wish for sentences
chosen by love:

Together we'll undress
my words and unfasten
my attachments.

Emptiness: (leave me alone)
I will not surrender to *blind faith*.

Earth breathes fear,
and most of humankind
is uncertain of *commandments*
in writing.

I shuffle my verbs, adverbs, contractions,
looking for instant gratification.

Disappointment:
Serious laughter,
like splinters in my throat;

I want to beg earth for forgiveness and
I am embarrassed for not knowing how.

Human kindness needs encouragement
(still our destruction will not be postponed).

How do we explain
to our children's children about
the darkness we are conjuring for them?

Nothing Of *God's* Origin

Nothing of *God's* origin
is known: To say this,

I must plunge into the universe,
shaking my soul clean of fear,
false-truth, ignorance, and misconception.

I must find this *old man*,
must find the seed to
his unexplained beginning.

I write these lines as
an invitation, a revelation,
an incantation

(letting them sprout from
my imagination). I am offering
my gratitude, my devotion,
my soul, in exchange for

a world free from uncertainty.

Death Is A Habit

Death is a habit filled with unknown presence,
invisible freedom, and empty beauty.

Life streaks through burning hearts and love
yet, life is not so dreadful:

Idleness is filled with tears and sloth is
a gesture of death.

Melancholy is death's splendid wine.
Depression is a deadly prescription.

Contentment is a curtain pulled back
allowing the mixture of life and death

to fuse into love [from one second to the next
we wait (sometimes unknowingly)

for the stranger
bearing black roses].

Death is a habit and life is
like a cigarette we burn through to get there.

Evidence: Clarity

Evidence: clarity's crimson
-colored light. Death says:

*Do not turn away from
the black roses that fill my hands.*

Solitude: A quiet so painfully
aching with joy—even

unspoken words become
disruptive, chattering about,
running underneath my tongue.

My cherished wealth:
Each blade of grass, each flower,
each tree branch, the birdbath

—all of this from my garden,
I am overly in love with.

Death says: *I have given you
a syllabus of hours, each
one is your life decaying.*

In the end,
earth will open her body,
and make love to my remains.

If I Ask The Dead For Memories

If I ask the dead for memories
then I must meditate on the
spirit-sound resonating in the sky where
the *Great Light* assures its majesty.

If I ask the dead to allow me
to enter the house of reliance,
where the future begins as a secret,
then I must meditate on a miracle
merely for a moment. This is

how I sustain: My living heat
quickens its flame as I observe
my deep breathing where

memory declares a subconscious self
and my human divinity thickens its soul,
like a heavy voice or a deep dream's density;

hours hasten and vanish, heavily cracked
and drowsy, jolted by the heart's last motion
—restless and wearied by each limping second.

If I meditate on death's sorrow then
I must cling to the shore of hesitation,
for tomorrow's unknown threatens the sun
that sears the sky: *My destiny whispers.*

If I meditate on the dead
then I must ask for their memories,
for the memories of my birth, for
the memories of my youth, and for
the memories of my mother and father:
Their souls are spiritual beacons.

It's like this: When the drifting sky turns
its vital mirror and my living reflection disappears
as death seals its vow across my lips, then

I must meditate on the radiant transformation
that no longer allows my eyes to see
and no longer allows my heart to beat.

The Singing From My Soul

The singing from my soul,
my limbs, my veins,
my breath, my pulse

—roaming the universe I realize:
There is no *God* greater than the *God* you are.

What is already known we must strip away
and stretch our flesh into speechless bliss.

I lay exposed, explaining myself:
My flame rushes my veins,
my breath accumulates light,
my limbs challenge death,
my pulse pumps erotically.

Endlessly folding and unfolding,
my body responds
with a yearning to celebrate.

Stretched-out in stillness,
I dream of light
lingering in my arms.

How sweet the silence,
only breathing.

The Order Of Ascension

If we follow the order of ascension
into *The Now* that expands its light
then we must believe in a far-off dawn's
luminous rise whose star sets fire to creation.

If a sound that we hear is the wind's instrument
teasingly stirring a cloud's splendid body, or the sky's
trumpet playing in the horizon's key, then we must
know that the moon's flute is an entrancing pleasure.

When we pass time's dust reflecting its illusion into
the mirrored certainty of infinity's magnificent arrangement,
then we must know that the star-filled distance possesses
a crowded ecstasy where spirits vibrate love's tempo:

Then, and only then,
will we understand *The Now's* living mind,
its power of conception, its phases of reality,
and our own *God-Power manifestation*

expressing eternal-realization.

Wet Thoughts For Thirsty Minds

Space is collective soul existing
without symptoms of time, and
every thing else—planets, moons, stars,
solar systems—is dense consciousness:
energized, coherent, and carnal.

Life agrees with energy's creative
sensibility and through this sensibility
life observes truth:

Who ever meditates from within
consciously inhabits veracity inside
the light of creation's endless awakening.

Nothing is real and all things are possible
—there's no difference here.

Perception fills itself with cycles of time
only to possess us with emotions, only to
define us through feelings, only to madden us
with metaphysical ignorance.

Spirit is as external as internal, as surreal as real,
as pure as purity: *Religion indicates that spiritual purity*
is soiled and that humanity is enslaved within
dictatorial control of mental assassins shooting
propaganda loaded with autocrat-designed fear;

religion is a societal myth endangering that which
is spiritually pure—mind expansion and free will.

To breathe is to belong to one another
by way of expansive freedom: We breathe
therefore we experience purity; we live therefore
we experience sensations; we die therefore
we are the eternal purity of *Elysium*.

In Need Of A Decent *God*

Dear *God*—Master of All,
the Seed, the Root, the Creator of Life,
the Heart of Soul and Love

—what has become of you with your
invisible absence? Why must I believe
in you and think of you as more, as
all things more, than myself?

Are we not the same essence? Energy?
Universal Force?

Am I not Us as Our image, as Our
physical manifestation here on earth
that we have designed together?

Are you not me as my image, as Love
and Infinite beauty? Tell me in your
own words and not in the words of that
man-made book: *If you are the Master Creator of Love*
then why have you left us in so much pain,

in so much emotional, spiritual, and physical pain,
for so many miserable millennia?
Are you happier this way?

Please, do not insult me, again, by telling me about
Lucifer turning his back on you, and that you need to
teach him a lesson, because I am exhausted on being
the whipping post for his alleged misjudgment. Ouch!

Show me dignity, respect, and intelligence.

My *god*, get a grip on reality!
Tell me something real. Make a noticeable effort
to show how loving you can be, and stop blaming
humanity's pain, destruction, and darkness on
Lucifer's Rebellion or on *Original Sin*:

It's unbecoming, exhausting, and indecent of you,
and I am a depraved poet in need of decency,
or maybe, in need of a decent *God*.

Twilight Is A Sudden Sadness

Who am I to know that
the existence of heaven lives
in the pause between breaths
or that the story of creation is
a searing scar in the side of *Jesus*?

I have collected my pleasures,
like monsoons collect the dead,
have collected my memories,
the raw force of vitality,

the swift silk of a spider's web,
the emptiness of being, all of this:
a country of vibrant emotions.

I have touched the sea with my hands,
bringing them together, feeling the abrupt
salt between my fingers, torrid like
the stinging whip of a lover:

Her tongue burns me alive with
its naked wine; her eyes dig
into the depths of mine.

Who am I to know that the *Kingdom of God*
lives in the stones, the fire, the water, the mud,
or that twilight is a sudden sadness like
gray blood clots caused by black thorns?

Still, my excitement is like a tower
of energy or a vigorous burst of sperm or
the moonlight's mysteries fitting its key
into my soul where a secret stillness

wallows in its swaggering bliss.
I have tasted the meat of the universe,
its heart, its lungs, its liver, tasting it
with my gentleness, a gentleness like

soft lips, or a feather, or a lover's whisper:
Her mouth burns me alive with its
raw juice; her heart feeds from mine.

Who am I to know that the *Supreme Spirit*
lives in the flies, the lice, the grub, or that
death's bitter sorrow lives in the dust, the bones,
the ash, or in the agony of a broken heart?

—once, *Jesus* summoned me. He undid
his wounds with the jagged blades of my
tears. I held him, embracing him, saying:

My brother, my brother, my peaceful brother…
who am I… to know…
who I am?

Upon The Fingers

Upon the fingers
of my left hand,

I count my wishes:
Peace. Love. Shelter.
Water. Food.

I sing, clearly, vibrating
and expanding my heart
center with contentment.

Each day I attempt
to laugh
a little more while

holding the smiles
of others
in my arms.

Day after day
I whisper to our injured earth,
apologizing for our *human clumsiness.*

I live counting the leaves
on all of the trees
—every leaf is my cousin.

When autumn's rain

brings them down
I will bury each leaf, reciting
(only) one word—*Love*

—only to water them with my beautiful tears
and bless them with my vigorous pulse.

I will press a fallen leaf
in between the pages of this book.

Years later I will come back to it
as if it were
an angel sleeping.

Hiding Behind Mythology

When will you, Angels,
make yourselves visible?

When will you stop hiding in shadows of mist, or behind
spiraling light beams?

I want to see your beauty, to touch your wings, to see unborn stars
in your eyes. And

if you truly carry *the answer* in your hearts, then I want a moment
with your hearts in my hands.

And if, Angels, your faces mirror the harmony of birth and death,
then I want a moment face to face with you—let me see this harmony.

If in your minds you have extinguished desire, then let me
press my head to your heads—let my desire die.

If upon your lips all of heaven's love gathers, then let me
press my lips to your lips—let me kiss you just once.

If from your stomachs, Angels, all creatures are set free,
then let me press my stomach to your stomachs—please, set me free.

If from your hair the sun rises and songs of birds are born,
then let me run my fingers through your hair—let me be born anew.

And when you arch your backs and rainbows spill across the sky,
then let me arch my back too! Let me spill rainbows!

Angels, if from your tongues all of creation flows, then let me
press my tongue to your tongues, just once—let me taste all of creation.

If only once, Angels, you would hold my hand so that your essence
would mix with my flesh, my blood, and bones—if only once.

Angels! When will you stop
hiding behind mythology?

Journal Entry: October 6th, 2006
4:AM Full Moon Coming: #63

This cold dark (as if inside a stone), I place my eyes against its grain,
there is no alien strangeness here, only that which is eroded
by time and empty of light. At this hour, its downdraft burns
from soul-salt, stranger than, more dense than, ravens circulating
their last breaths. My eyes drag across this muted hour
covered in moist-threaded-grayish clouds, dragging blurred
retinas, body-bones, blood-chill—I shiver near a steamed pane.

Gasping, already, I am gasping at the sight of nothing: *IT* shines
from my memory-grove (before I knew *IT*; before *IT* opened me;
before blood poured warm, before my mouth opened, crying).

Is the inside of a stone blind or an insomniac eyeball without flesh?

My hands reach into morning's dark fabric, scooping nothing
in their movement: empty air only my lungs are in love with;
my fingers swim through a sleepless dream-wonder of silent puddles,
air puddles—heaven must be gray at this hour above
a nothingness of cloud-brains so thick with storm; the sea sails
its salt skyward; mud-reeds dwell there along the wet drifts,
remaining nimble anyway.

My soul aches an unmistakable ache (you know the one),
a blackened ache from my thoughts beating it with wordless,
soundless, opinionated clubs, a flurry of them

—a hurricane-like breathing interrupts me every time
I get close enough to know the soft words of silence.
Stones know, don't they? They live an uninterrupted
silence, gladly living in silence:

not a deaf silence, rather, in a gloriously-silent-satisfaction.

Where light formed for us before breath, angels flew backwards
only to glance at *IT* hitting the infinite souls of those to be born (again?).
IT saw us before when we were *still-dust* existing from nothing, over and
over again from nothing—*whose dust?*— plunged, floated, drifted,
joined together.

Without eyes we were, all of us, blind dust:

by a cosmic kiss

and mys

tical copu

lation *IT*

entered us

deeply

our inhal

ations

wet with *IT*

IT in us

awak

ened

the ero

tic feathers

of love-

pulsing.

From certain points straight into the wind, I thought I would understand the depth of the universe with its leisurely enlightenment

—lightning returns *intense and swift;* planets assemble storms; light veers into the sea; the sea's delicate spray

—only to realize,

we must amuse ourselves with what ourselves have.

Tonight, the towering illumination of nocturnal energy hemorrhages its miracle and brims with quiet chaos as wide-open as any enigma allows.

I move my shadow (with its useless chemistry) under a flood of candlelight, only to be astonished by its unimaginable easiness in remaining comfortable—no matter what.

Seeking my own elementary comfort, I discovered that rest is nothing without first having restlessness; that strength is nothing without first having weakness; that sadness and loneliness are lifted by a true understanding of the purity in polar opposites;

one without the other will never be pure:

Self-inflicted sadness
is neither right nor wrong,
it's simply empty,
and tragically visionless.

Self-inflicted sadness is nowhere and to dwell on it creates the perfect spiritual crime: creates death without graves; creates a sky that ends abruptly, or a wound that never heals, or a ghost that is not invisible.

At this moment (Four AM) the city lies in darkness, a stormy, wet darkness that autumn hardens with its chill

—this dark light is like black powder
floating into dense shadows

—the sea outside my window
pursues its rise

—garden luscious is ravaged
by the deluge, along
one of her paths

the scent of lavender
quiets itself.

In the end we'll comprehend that eternity's eternal-bliss
had never left us—it was simply buried under our human ignorance.

October Passes

October passes,
I drink the air
and tighten my scarf.

Purple sky forms
over the Golden Gate bridge,
the cold freezes the last figs.
I remember doves nesting
outside my window, now

clouds gather chaos.
November's skepticism
(already)
brings fear to the shadows.

The weather: A furious *god*
—I pray for change.
My confession:
Light is my happiness.

I hear vaporous rain gathering in the grazing clouds, all of them, made of sleeping prisms. Wind rushes as if it needs to go farther, rushes up a staircase, like a lighthouse beam bound in its wet skin.

I try not to protect the full moon—it's pointless—the storm will snuff it into a candle flame's ghostly smoke (which always smells of pungent church breath).

Last night I ventured so far into a dream and, as ecstatic as I was,
I kept racing back to the edge of reality, feeling dawn licking
my eyes: Each day my fondness for morning is the joy of
opening a new presence.

Dawn: Your glowing foliage, your panoramic light-swells,
all of this, bubbles in front of my eyes. I rise like a cock,
a big, feathery cock with a red head glowing, crowing, crowing
at your tender outline, at the slowness of yawns,
at my vigorous virility. It's a blessing to be alive!

If needed, I could gather the chattering birds with their poetic
fountains of sound, gather them into a feathered necklace,
and give each one a pet name.

My nightmares are in revolution. If I show my face they will cut
my mind out of my soul. When nightmares come I hide, sometimes
under the covers. If they find me I may never see the future again
or visit the ruins of memory.

Nightmares have banded together searching me out.
I carry a *light-beam-sword* sharp as any visionary and
I watch that my heart doesn't slam shut:
Nightmares feed on the insides of closed hearts.

WINTER

With storms so livid and coated with ice, even the wings of ducks, their feet, and their bills forget how to function, and in the lair, deep in mahogany dreams, the bears snore like symphonic tubas.

Outside Only A Few Sounds

Outside, only a few sounds
remain from the rain.

The sea's edge
throws the debris
from industry at the seagulls

—standing on one leg,
a sense of danger
is not in their imaginations.

I listen to the sea:
What is contentment?

I doubt these words
will carry a message,
I write them anyway:

What is contentment?

I write slowly as if stuck
in a misguided dream
while asking each word
to explain itself

—the voices of these words
are smooth and sleepy,
unspoken like silent wolves.

I watch them form
living verbs, obscured nouns,
quivering contractions,
enormous certainty, and

reciting their loyalty:
What is contentment?

My words breathe
like a night nurse that cares
for comatose patients.

Time nods at the evening
to put me to sleep:

My soul is burning.
Between my fingers,
time is still.

Time:
a street I've walked before
—the bare trees; the nervous darkness;
the lips of strangers; a dog's tongue hangs out.

Silence: a ringing in my left ear
like a distraught child screaming for its mother.
What is contentment?

Gospel 1:1 Big Sur Coast

At a certain pitch the ocean holds me
spellbound, defining no limit to beauty;

a mirrored reflection layers the sea—clouds,
sun, birds, a blue interior; an abundance of life underneath.

Light filters color, passing passively. My eyes, calm
along the distance: The horizon satisfies, pleases, and makes no sound.

Without instruction, I travel the beach (understanding
its vital information): A wave explodes and escapes the sea

only to realize
its rebirth into light and air.

Today's unseasonable warmth primes my blood with various
heat waves: Summer, hot springs, volcanoes, the tropics.

I see someone, a naked man: a stranger, holding stillness
in his stance, facing southeast. Illuminated. Recharging.

His back is to me: winter's cold water like wet socks
around his bare ankles. Foam clings.

I bow to him and ask to be forgiven for my ignorance. He stands
in a trance and, floating into the sky, vanishes, as if nothing.

I sit in meditation and pause my breath long enough
to understand how delicate peace is.

3:AM INSOMNIA

The streets are as still as dead bones; the dark kisses
my eyes, then licks its chilled, black tongue over my skin
—this expression of emptiness (like a vivid mirror convulsing
into drawn-out lifelessness) is existing and defined.

I go to the window, only because I cannot sleep, only
to add a teardrop to the rain's sadness, only to witness
more emptiness than I am feeling, which makes me feel full:

Loneliness itself is a living tomb, an empty hallway,
a long, empty staircase leading to a vacant temple where
God's body lies in death's creepy cold stillness

—looking at him, I see the entire world, everybody, everywhere,
in gut-wrenching emotional pain. I yell at him: *You have left us here*
as spiritual orphans with only fantasies and unfulfilled, drawn-out
promises for us to hold faith in. Humanity is your biggest mistake!

Suspended in this flighty, clenching thought, the wind against
the trees grounds my feelings—my heart begins to run backwards
to the beginning, to that luscious garden, to the *Tree Of Knowledge,*
where I feel *God's* heart beating inside of my body,

only to realize that it's my heart beating, that I am (as all
of us are) *the gods of our own lives,* and the whole of all
universal knowledge is one part of who we are. I hold this
thought along the great distance of my certainty, touching
solitude within the suddenness of my own mystical awakening.

Now, at 4:AM, again,

I am looking out of the window and it appears that the rain

has created one-huge-tear filled with winter's sadness, and

the long, sloth-like movement of the hour-hand deepens

my craving for another mug of hot coffee, then I write

what I am instructed to write:

I seek more than what I have been told to believe in

—shh … listen … here comes another transmission of *Truth*

grinding its gears and breaking across the clear field of

my understanding. Finally, the sky has drained its last sadness and

I hear contentment folding its wings into transfigured breathing,

and *The Light* shines (not on me but) from within me.

Let Me Speak Of *God*

Let me speak of *God*: Never is his response
to humanity's miseries

—his absence, his arrogance,
his indifference.

It freezes me in tears to think of such
illuminated selfishness in possession of everything.

I view the entire religious scene as diabolical torture,
the wearing down of one soul after another.

My blasphemous confession: *a dangerous freedom*
harboring reckless abandon and spiritual freewill.

I fall to my knees and raise my head to the sky
asking for: *Love! Love! Love!*

What love is there in the death of a still-born,
or in the crippling of a child, or in
the creation of the Monsters Of Genocide?

Let me flip my thoughts to
the mysterious scents that shake my soul.

I keep these lines close to the unbreakable light
sailing with my blood.

My divine verse: to transmigrate
in the name of love.

Until that moment, I lower my eyes in disbelief
—giving birth: *Mary was not virgin.*

I hold these words on my tongue,
putting no obstacles in the way of their vibration:

to be *sane with love,* fat, flowering love; fragrant,
fingering love; enormous winged love

—I should be *God*! Or you! Or You! Or You!

the Creator is us

For a long time, near the beginning,
I have faced southeast contemplating
its vast energy force as a conductor
for the *Light Beam's* subterranean consciousness.

Gazing southeast, I understand that
the dazzling *Light Beam's* radiance,
its pure divine essence is, nothing more
or less than, my own spiritual purity.

It's like this: *From beneath mountains of dogma*
and zealous worshippers, I crawled out and
into the revelation of self, into the joyfulness of inner-power,
into the expansion of imagination, thoughts, and creation.

This revelation led to unconditional love
found in the heart of Universal Soul:
energy being all of us, together, as one.
Mystical probing took me into Soul
(the subterranean consciousness), into
Stillness and Silence: where nothing
is expressed and everything is
the sensation of existence.

It is as simple as this: *Fear has broken wings;*
greed is a cry of loneliness; despair is
an empty heart; hate is a suffocating mouth;
and dogma is deceitful cant.

With space expressing undeniable eternity,
I sit facing southeast in *Stillness and Silence*,
absorbing truthful transmissions: *Everything
-is-always-forever-one-love.*

Thoughts are vital active energy:
Only ignorance to this keeps us caged
—change our thoughts and the cage is gone;
who we are we have created. the Creator is us.

The Wild Mud Of Sleep

I feel the growth of the universe,
its living roots, its coming and going, and
the moon unwinds, dragging its cold, dead kingdom
around earth's vigorous magnetic pulsing:

Today I watched a red hawk burn a gray sky,
as if a flame or a spear, searing the air
with its vicious hunger, seeking nourishment

—as the trees are sensitive, brittle, and swallowed
by winter's bitterness I, too, feel the empty lamp
of the hidden sun within the chill's fullness.

In another vision: *I saw the Ancients alone*
with earth and wind, with the ancient waters,
without asking for more, and a fire the color
of sunset, ceremonial wings, blood, and spirit.

The ravenous red hawk hunts, pursues,
and the air is turbulent with fear,
then stillness, then silence.

The north wind is like a blunt object
hitting me in the face with its cruel touch,
its fingers like icicles; this wintry day has

hurriedly eaten its way through the light, has
eaten its way into the assembled shadows
asleep in the dark, only to arrive at

the fortune of transfigured dreams,
where the dark hours gather
the wild mud of sleep
upon my eyes.

The Atmosphere's Vibration

...a slice of buttered toast; a mug of black coffee,
and the morning sits down with me, dignified
by its tinted red dawn.

The hours proceed without effort, understanding
the exhausted little hand's slow crawl:
The hours force nothing but their own labor.

This splendid morning's fruitful promise
breaks into several octaves of telescoping
silence, as if the clouds were monks in red robes
pondering the atmosphere's vibration. Silently.
Pondering:

What's all of this got to do with me?
Why am I living and dying at the same time?
Why would *Jesus* have wept for me when
the spikes pierced his hands, crushed his bones?
Pondering. Thoughts. Feelings. Beliefs:

The chaos of mind knows no order,
only to be chaotic without order.

To say that one's mind is empty in meditation
is to not know one's mind.

The empty space through which a thought passes
is no longer empty.

Human Happiness: an energetic child dazzled by
the arrival of new dawns, new hopes, and dreams.

Human Unhappiness: the lowest form of existence
inhabited by melancholy's numbness.

Loneliness: a sharp stick broken of off the Tree Of Life
and stuck into the heart.

—in between my thoughts a body of emptiness
takes pleasure in its own enigma.

I drink my coffee and feel the caffeine clawing at my nerves,
my heart races; my body heats up—damn, not my twisted beliefs,
again, looking for trouble:

Life without one's own belief system is idle spiritual growth, an illusion
that there is something more to believe in than one's self.

Show Me Something Invisible

Pushing my memory, pushing further, seeking *something*
deeper within the heat of my living pulse: I've pondered my birth,
here, in this body, whose spirit is a phantom from another dimension
feeding on breath, blood, bones, and organs.

My astral longing takes wing to distant pleasures, sensual
and loving; soars into spiritual light, free from atonement,
or helplessness: *This light leaks out of my heart and
into every cell of my naked interior, its vital beam
places glorious visions upon my thirsty mind.*

I have whispered at what is not there, drawing myself
closer to the unique creature of my being, here, alive,
yet time washes me older with its invisible waves
stinging each birth wound, only to remain a stranger,
here, pushing my memory, which keeps a profound,
shallow silence.

Between pain and pleasure there is a dimension that
is neither living nor dead, that is neither the beginning
nor the end—Infinity! Eternity! Forever?

Because of breath I can feel life's precious order:
Desire. Crave. Hunger. —and the climbing of my skeleton
underneath my skin has made me taller, older, and wiser. Wiser?

Life's temporal weight reminds me that there's *something* lighter,
something brighter, *something* invisible. Oh memory! Show me
something invisible! *Something* infinitely invisible to believe in
because *Faith* is simply a word, only a simple word,
tethered to trepidation, ignorance, and helplessness
—I possess none of these. Now, *show me something invisible*
to believe in.

Sorrow's Dangerous Death-Blade

This day unloads its cracked clouds,
its chaos and madness, forging its downpour
through the shivering air, one squall upon another,
announcing itself as *God's* sickness: Each deformed
cloud is a humpback of winter's dark anxiety.

A flying wind, something of illusion's wings,
flaunts its agony as if a suicidal-finger pressing
a trigger or engraving the sky with sorrow's
dangerous death-blade:

Oh such colossal sobbing, slanted veins of rain,
sacrificial ground, all of this, wounded by
a sacred mourning coming from the elements.

Suddenly, a deep thought:
My soul has rescued my dreams because,
bestowed upon me, keeper of the *Heart-Light*,
are duties existing through eternity's burning
faith in my being and non-being.

I shape myself for you, immense and mythological,
for you to remain my divine fuel, gasping at my
perennial flame while my relentless heat
is a slave to your faithful heartbeat.

Return from deep thought:
This day's eyelashes, so sad and tear weathered,

knock this winter-hour cold as if chains fastened
to a skeletal graveyard and rusted around trees
drunk on dismal light.

Forgive me, but the Pacific's cruel seasonal
enthusiasm makes evil laugh out loud with
its hissing-like-nervous-feline-energy pounding
swift pain into coastal decay, debris, seashells
and seabirds. Footprints in the sand
stand no chance of surviving.

common sense is My Savior

Oh sweet light covering my divine body,
invisible, blinding, returning me
to my original self, raw and powerful.

I remain silent, reclining along the shore,
the sea; the rising air; my breath;
a light breeze as if spirits with
warm smiles spill over my heart.

I, animal, man, lover, praise the universe
that I, you, *all of us*, have created and formed;
it gushes forth with our light, our glorious
light, resurrecting truth buried in our hearts
for all to see, love, hold, know and live:

What I say and think is understood as nothing
but creation, dark and light, hot and cold
—a relief to some, disconcerting to others. Listen:

Oh luminous souls put your hallowed books down
and stop suffering the musty torment of those
delusional, dead apostles; shout, drum, dance,
fuck, and live, till your earth-light blows out.

I have done nothing wrong, nothing
but believing in myself and you
and the decency and indecency

in living without sin, confusion, or regret
—common sense is my savior.

This freedom leaves me in tears, joy, laughter,
leaves me courageous and spiritual and
out of the clutches of dogmatic domination
—oh that stale, useless suffering; society's lingering
illness; a black spot on the heart and soul of earth;
a wolf in sheep's clothing.

Intuition is my *god*, my vessel, my guiding light:
The search is over.

Masters Of Energy

A realized vision reappears as if soothing lips, or wholesome saints,
place golden kisses upon my soul:

Divinity (with all of our glorious powers along the prism of
the moon's edge) has set serenity free to gather the dancers and lovers,

to gather the wonders of the present, to gather
the great light of shadow makers, and

I feel, again, the fever in my dreams, hot and aroused,
full of Utopian froth, rhythms of undulant orgasms, while sun-filled days

pulsate with the sounds of singing charms. I hear celebrations
with great masses of eyes, with tears so utterly aligned with jubilation,

and time and space copulate with reality,
immortality, magic, life and death.

I have no time for doubt, no time for fear, no time to hate, or to deny
that your existence is anything but my existence—*our existence*.

Forever is immortality's passion for eternity. Love hears us,
feels us, embraces us, with the perfect proportion of contentment

coming from our mind's infinite designs:
All things come from within; love does not resist.

I see mornings alive with ambitious red clouds,
like fantastic banners, or fragments of fire, and

the sea moans incessantly as each wave
cradles its own soul's ecstatic love:

We come from within projecting outward,
masters of energy, bringing breath to body,

bringing soul to mind, bringing mind to consciousness,
bringing body to life, life to death, and forever to eternity.

Through The Channels

Through the channels,
the horns, the paths,
we have come, all of us,
as if over-night,

as if lifted above the mountains'
mouths, or the moon's lantern
—what carried us here
from there,

what space-sperm, light beam,
or energy-echo?
Through the uncircumcised life-line
we have come, all of us,

in the mornings
and evenings:
our memories
empty of *IT*.

The Spirituality Of A Rainbow

The spirituality of a rainbow:
a colorful thought from
universal consciousness
manifesting across the sky.

The living colors of water and light
illuminating, silently, as if
a wisp of innocent beauty
from eternity's memory

—smearing, stretching, arching,
its raw finish, its vibrant nakedness,
for all of creation to delight in.
I bow to the ephemeral visits

of rainbows,
to their
fleeting impressions of
luminous spirit.

A Shawl Of Indigo Aura

The evening is a thick, black lid
closing over the sun:
Tonight the sky is inlaid
with pink clouds

because the light has crawled
inside of them falling asleep.
How is it
I understand light's recital,

yet have no words to
explain it?
A poem without words?
A poet without a voice?

Today I watched a child,
a young girl, my daughter,
stepping into a puddle of light.
She said: *I have sailed here before.*

Her breath has the weight
of a sparrow. Her eyes, like poetry itself.
She wears a shawl of indigo aura
and gives me armfuls of her enthusiastic love.

My seven-year-old daughter, with a plum-tree stick
in her hand, saving earth worms from drowning
—winter storms have destroyed their homes

—her enthusiastic love was saving them:
Bellies down, she placed the exhausted
earth worms in the grass, quietly talking to them.
To the dead ones she whispered:
I love you and have a wonderful after-life.

Of the darkness: Together we whispered
about light falling asleep.

The Only *God* I Need

The sea, with its never-ending waves like soft warriors each one,
drums its monsoon dream, thick and truthful, while gulping
light into their silvery mouths.

Sitting in full lotus, I observe my breath while searching for
warm tones and spiritual harmony; a mystical thirst draws silence

from the air's breath; sea salt drinks from my lips,
and everything is primal like the sun before time: Silence
speaks without sound, witnessing

my stillness—I am born, each second of my life,
born from the pure slowness of my inhales infusing

light particles into my lungs with divine ecstasy.
The sea speaks with a lover's command
or with the force of a gentle storm and

I feel her delicate mist, like explosions of
raw kisses, wild with salt and sand.

A deep-winter's metallic light falls near
evening's on-coming black foliage,
and joy fills my vessel, my bones,

blood, lungs, my heart, with an unbreakable peace
alive near the sea's turbulent beauty;
dreamy; drifting; suddenly eternal;

filling me with the unfiltered substance of

universal-prana.

I sit in full lotus,

holding the key to nothing, holding the key to nowhere,

knowing: The only entrance to myself is from within;

the only God I need to find is myself.

Let Us Make Peace

Come, and let us make peace with the sea,
approaching each wave as a temple or an altar;
sometimes I listen for no reason other than
awareness, or to exchange feelings, comfort,
or understanding: What affects the soul?

Every dream is a thought or a messenger,
some dressed in memories not yet fully
functional because the pain of recall may be
too emotional, or a matter of taste.

The sea's joint-less body escapes
into the sand leaving traces of raw salt
disinfecting earth's pain—earth
takes this mineral and divides it between
sun and air where moisture becomes
a passageway for rainbows.

In the body of sky above and below
existence is a mirrored reflection deeply
connected to the sea, connected by
a passing of light that, at sunset,
burns into a dark pause:

What affects the soul—belief in self,
or belief in eternal consciousness?

The stars, like explosive ornaments,
force their fire, intertwining the moon
with dust and light. Creation.

Between the waves are alleyways for seagulls
to fly through—the wind presses against
their feathers, bound by space, and
runs its tempo inside my heart.

The waves break with an ancient breathlessness
and seek higher ground by reaching for heaven
with their tears, only to fall back. Forgetting.

Come: *Let us make peace with the sea, the earth,*
the air, the sky, and the light. Let us disarm hate
so we can play and exist. Together.

The Sea

The Sea was childless.
Yes! Yes!

The Sea was childless—that is,
before I came, before I saw the curve
of space between the waves and
a slice of blue in a dolphin's eyes,

where the splendid star mirrors itself
in billows of salt; where the surf
swallows the sand 'til grains of salt
and sand remember how to laugh
together.

Look!
The Sea has settled the conflict
between the air and light
caught in its mouth.

Along the shore I chased sandpipers
'til they fell into the holes they pecked,
where their eyes caved-in like frightened
still-lives, and salt filled their hunger

(I cried at the sight of decay before
the sea offered it to its drowned, before
I understood: Decay is the sea's food).

I offer myself to the sea, not as a madman,
or a dancer of the whip that burns the tip
of the sun, but as a child of the sea.

I offer myself:
to the air and light that mixes with saltwater.

To the voice of the sea:
I offer my lungs.

To the dense moisture of waves:
I offer my salted tears.

To the assurance of the drowned:
I offer my heart.

To the delicate songs of somersaulting whales:
I offer my voice.

To the living sky's divine substance:
I offer my eyes.

To the mouths of hungry sea creatures:
I offer my flesh and bones.

To the joy of holding a child in my heart:
I give myself completely.

In waves In rocks

In waves, in rocks,
the salt astride the wind
—to the air this is nothing.
I raise my heart

in hope of reaching a final horizon.
The sea is filled with blessings,
coral rises, the sky sails on
[the helm of my spirit

(that which is greater
than a distant universe)
was not done by *God*].
I lift my hands, holding

earth's spinning soul
(time has come; time has gone;
time has life, joy, death).
Encircling the primal mother

(with both hands motioning to her),
time dribbles away.
If *God* flashed his view on this,
it's nowhere to be seen.

My soul's strength is
the force silence is made from

—I suspend this thought
within the sharpness of a vision:

Having unlocked heaven (I've
done this before), death's
eclipse (its massive empire)
returns, looking for my soul

—within the contour of space,
my breath will dissolve to Utopian-Silence.

Much Older Now

Much older now: I have returned to my soul,
holding earth's stained skin in my hands.

A great illusion is in front of me,
the sky spreads its moons;

time is dying yet never stops creating
and destroying life.

I have spoken of perfect hours, the accomplishments of years,
unfaithful silence, a rush of salt from the seas.

In this world the sky is a poet and the whole of life
inhales dawn and dusk—consider this:

Love:
a meeting place upon our mouths.

Loneliness:
a shadow a body no longer owns.

Love:
Give me your hand
and feel my breath spill over.

Harmony:
a hidden sweetness; the sky's silence;
a piece of love from a finished kiss.

Nocturnal Love:
a wildly scented bonfire; shadows
against emptiness; sunlight
held by the moon.

Winter's Light:
a fresh wound of deep moisture;
a transformation of air to glittering rain;
a mouth that sings like a banjo.

Under layers of life, death rots to its very end.
Life has set fire to us—we must burn.

The Stars Embroidered My Soul

An end-of-the-day easiness swirls around me
in a ballet of living energy: Evening falls warmly
against dark light mixing a meditative candle glow
with deep shadows.

I do not know if I exist or do not exist, nor does it
matter; I see reality as if for the first time, every time,
and I am enchanted by light, like morning glories that climb
toward the sun and pull their heavy vegetation with them.

All of reality lives before me, surrounds me,
within a dark moon's peacefulness—this is
a moment and nothing more: Tonight

the red sunset quivered into a pale, white corpse
of tranquil silence and, for a moment, possessed me
as if my soul suffered from loneliness or madness
—only for a moment.

I am not a believer in much except for the imperfect
nervous system of energy's existence whose irregular
attitude manipulates our atmosphere's consciousness
into a current of swift electrical charges of comfort
and discomfort—this is reality.

The passing of oxygen in and out of my body
entrances me; the monotony of eating is a flaw
an imperfect *god* has left us with; the surreal

order of dreams is, at times, a suffering relief
from life's material-hunger—only sometimes.

My mind contains images of earth's magnetic body
empty of humanity's brutal vigor. I group my thoughts,
searching for complete sentences that I can feel:

*A paragraph forms, then another, and another, until
a poem is born, breathing, and hungry, leaving me with the
obligation to feed it with more thoughts until it is confident
enough to live and express on its own.*

Before I was born the stars embroidered my soul with fire,
creating enough light for me to find my way:
Upon a light beam, I arrived.

Under A Sky Of Dreamy Dreams

Under a sky of dreamy dreams,
over the light of my soul,
caught in the order of faith
(my mind, my imagination,
my reasons):

I own everything divinity has
—the power of darkness; the opening
of dawn; the whole day's return
—surviving on survival itself.

Facing sorrow
(lingering on its own)
beyond myself,
I wait patiently for joy:

My endurance is plain, and
blindness dreams for reasons to see.

Everyone's primal memory
screams like a natal cry
—I hold kisses in my hands,
rubbing them on memory's lips.

Mortality
is everything death wants
—I post this across the sky,
and looking into the eyes

of love, I know that
being alive is a glorious
gathering of energy, and

each new wrinkle
is a path to eternity.

I Wake Up Dreaming

I wake up dreaming and keep dreaming
to keep from screaming out loud while

composing long verbs for speaking to the dark
at four in the morning.

In the midst of the black light, then the blue light
(surrounded by

cold stillness, estranged thoughts,
dead air, and aching tendons),

the brittle windows'
icy cheeks surround the house.

Asleep near my feelings,
delight has pulled its curtains tightly;

the dark sleeps hard against winter's harsh air,
and memory is begging for a celebration

(its lower lip petitioning
stories, flavors, pieces of joy).

I sit up straight so as not to forget the trees
(thanking them for this paper).

Writing (my lines are as rough as bark,
as sloppy as a soggy sky).

Writing from a dream-reel: *Finding my pulse,
my heat, my soul searches this pulp for itself,*

*for a poem that doesn't smell
of human decay.*

Clutching the skin of heaven (this is still a dream),
I smell the stench of humanity rising,

its weight crushes the atmosphere,
its breath smells of furious conflicts.

As I read these lines to myself, I begin to write
in a language no longer disquieting:

*From the soul of my soul I find myself
in a place where memory has never been.*

I can't explain this and
there is an opening here

only it's empty and silent
and composed of solitude.

I understand emptiness,
it's composed of itself.

Emptiness wears no sandals,
walking barefoot over dead silence.

It opens its body, its stomach,
all of humanity is in there aching for deliverance:

Lord, we have given you thousands of years of blind faith,
still you do not comfort our delicate hearts in your loving hands.

To understand this, I must tear out
all of the pages of the *holy books,*

so the emptiness (from cover to cover)
will be as real as death and dust, and

fear will lose its features, its self-importance,
its misunderstandings.

My soul is at the foundation of a vision,
only, this vision is built upon

the erasable lines of this dimly lit poem.
Speaking of this vision, I speak for my self:

All life, God, change it or end it.
I listen for a response, but

there is a dead silence,
like a *god* that doesn't exist.

SPRING

A tender singing of choral harmony; the pleasant company of cozy shadows; a season of whispering light, and a breath of delicate breeze coming warm out of the south.

i am

i am
in all form
the embodiment
of reality's truth
the physical moment
of
creation's dream
manifested
from
the invisible
illusion of space
to the visible
light charged
energy
of reality
i am
therefore
reality is
too

I Pour My Bright Soul

I pour my bright soul
(glimmering with light)
into a heavenly spring's
flame-flung froth.

And like a large *god*
or a modest Buddha,
my bright soul's lightning
bolt (safe and snug
in the *Mother Womb*)

is divinity's perfection,
infinity's beauty,
a living star: *Love!*

Love opens
worlds, universes, stars,
beyond sight and sound,
and no darkness
is clever enough
to stay forever dark.

My soul's gifted sparkle
never forgets to bathe in light
—nothing else matters but
the ethereal orgasmic rush
from bathing in light.

Coaxing My Soul Into The Open

The moon layers ceremonial beams
into my eyes, and the marble light's
white veil cascades the night
with a mystical mist moving

over
the rising sea's throttled waves
against the air's juicy salt.

And sometimes I want to lift
earth's skin, lift it up, peel it back,
only to get closer to her nerves,

only to walk upon the bracelets
of her minerals to the hidden places,
to the secret light, to where the Ancients
left their magic and their blood.

My mouth opens to the center of
this night-wind quilted with
sand and salt, and like a ghostly scar,
the mist appears to be gesturing for empathy
or immortality.

And I see the broken-down lap of
a coastal Juniper, cold and damaged,
burning from the stinging salt and

bitter sand—its meaningful death
is food for earth's skin.

Everything about earth is all I need—
her slow scent from a wholesome wilderness
stretches across my stomach, heart, lungs,
and ribs, coaxing my soul into the open.

The Moisture Of My Soul

In the magnified whiteness of a morning cloud
(a cloud like a fortress), the rippled heat's rising sun
is lustful and hot, over done with spring's fever;
the cloud's whole shape (like angelic script)
spills white across an ethereal blue cloth.

Everything is splashed with warm, lemon light
as if *God's penis is dripping* and running through
the air and across the smooth page of this glorious
morning (still half dreaming, I am not fully awake).
At the edge of the hour a longing to live

this day, to lift into the parting lips of dawn,
to ascend my gaze along the airy trails of
flying birds—I rise into the infinite surrealism
of another moment's reality: Tracing the sky
with my eyes, the repeating rhythm of

gathering light-waves (like wings of tranquility)
slip over the treetops, spilling onto the fertile
earth of the garden, over a multitude of colorful
flowers looking like translucent paper cutouts.
Everything is a precise verse of seasonal expression,

unfolding, arriving, with such imagination and
downy weightlessness, awe-inspiring, a beautiful dizziness
of fresh light and birds, together, filling the sky: to have

my bare feet upon earth; the garden in full aroma;
the diaphanous green leaves of spring; a warm, gentle breeze;

to see the garden naked and unashamed, nourishing
her body with minerals and water; to see dawn's
blue eyes; her lips, parting with the essence of
surreal-reality; to feel her rising heat stimulating
the moisture of my soul.

My Soul Puts Its Eye To The Keyhole

My soul puts its eye to the keyhole,
so, like in every secret heaven,

God's laziness can be seen
(his simple game
is counting prayers
and more prayers,
then laughing)

—my soul's light-miracle,
I recognize its illumination,
its full wings:

I am chanting and repeating
chanting and chanting again

(asking for strange flames
to open my escape).

My soul, with its eye
to the keyhole: Silence roars!

I sharpen this thought
on dawn's sparkling rush

(her perfect breasts
cupped in my hands).

My soul
(its clear perfection
fueled by stars)

wants to sharpen its vision
by re-entering my primal dream:

A passionate sea's voice
is harmonized by the songs of whales
—I must return. There.

Light Passes Through Us

Light passes through us,
coloring our eyes

—then we can see.

When we die
the light above us does not go out.

Creation does not die, does not
stop its commotion.

When we die,
light passes through us,

and we can see, again:
The *Genie* is *us*

—rise to universal mind!

There is no hell growing black tulips in need
of watering—there is only eternity's light.

I Want Truth

I want truth
with all of its visions:

To think about this
I must possess
the emptiness of dried oceans.

Between nothing and everything
my soul, my fire, bows
to this order of realities:

The world is woven of dreams
(more real than spiritual fantasies).

God's absence is unfaithful love.
False-Truth is a pretentious mortal.
Seeing (all of) this in writing

I draw my senses inward,
protecting my living feelings
from tenacious religious scriptures.

Religion: This will not save us.

If we were to stretch our minds to another universe,
our consciousness would duplicate our souls
—this would be our work of genius.

Memory Derailed

An open window: Winter's last remaining light
lingers on the sill, prying apart spring's
eyes; a sparrow arises, ascends
—deep shadows from small wings.

Empty is the sky; blue crystal
in clear ether; cloudless;
a lovely distraction; mind-flinging
thoughts adjusting to the formless.

Wide-awake I am eating away at life
—a vital ray of energy caught in all of
its beauty—*I am a flame, a prism,*
a god sweeping through.

A drowsy tranquility of stillness
follows winter's last rain (that washed
spring's face); a pathway emerges,
along which the flowers half-open.

Enchanted, absorbed; I am mesmerized
by the fluttering of a swallowtail's flight
passing upon the warm air, like an angel
whose substance is impossible silence.

My eyes fill with light as if
savages with torches, exploding,

daydreaming, wrapped around
seasonal flowers, only to realize:

Creation shows me wonders,
like the order of life—yet recall,
at the moment of birth,
is empty and

memory is derailed
in less time than a natal cry.

Upon The Tender Leaves Of Spring

Upon the tender leaves of spring the sun leaves its face
like a copper ocean smearing some far-off horizon with
a bright linear smile, and

in the vivid blue, a living cloud crawls along the wind's hair
and trembles like a wet pearl, then pauses, momentarily,
as if a dream waiting for its thoughts.

Walking barefoot along the shore I turn sand dollars over
with my naked toes, and the saltiness of the sea's body
pursues me, sticking to my skin

as the heavy waves soak and grip the coast with their
whole bodies against the sand's captivity: A seagull's
voice loosens its pitch and

saturates the air with its poetic essence rising above
the ocean's thunderous crescendos that melt into
the slow breath of a lovemaking adagio.

I breathe in, deeply, the existence of earth's truth, her blood,
and bones, her roots, stones, and fire, breathe in deeply
her salt into my salt, and her soul she gives to me

as I give my soul to her—I close my eyes, only to taste
her on my lips, only to hear her whispering through
the sand in a voice that softly sways my heart.

Suddenly, a vision: *I see the Ancients coming at*
dawn under a still-sleepy sky, embracing the air's pure
linen, and piling logs onto a ceremonial fire;

raising their arms to the horizon, they chant and dance
in a clockwise circle around the blazing flames, then back,
then clockwise, and again the other way, until the sun shows

its full entrance into the morning sky—then they
throw burning sage leaves into the air only to sit
and meditate in silence. I breathe their purity.

SUMMER

Desserts of sizzling heat and a thirst for lemonade, with bronzed dancers and bohemian lovers in slow verses at dawn under sultry light and a blue enameled sky absorbing all of the birds.

I Praise The Morning Loudly

Light is the inner-urge of stars singing out
at the living request of dawn, and all of
dark's destruction is repaired by a single beam:

It's morning, come and feed, dragonflies
and butterflies, bury your mouths in each little
wildflower and soak up the crystal weeping dew;
leap from petal to petal; place your eggs upon
each color and rub your wings in harmony.

Earth smells good! And tastes even better!
She is raw and alive with nutrients and minerals
for me to rub my face into, and I am kissed on
the back of my head by the sun's great grin.

It's morning; the sky has built its blue spread
printed with puffy white and a breath of breeze
to set sail by. Listen! The mourning doves and
mockingbirds hold mouths full of melodies
mystical enough to be little *gods*.

I am wide-awake now with my barefoot toes
loving each blade of wet green, my eyes are
feverish for nature's nakedness, and my ears
hold animal sounds close to my heart.

Oh, look! A red fox sits at the edge of the meadow,
its curiosity aimed at me; a red hawk ropes the air

with its tail feathers streaming, and a mule deer
bolts into the forest at the sound of my song:

> *I praise the morning loudly,*
> *I praise it loud and clear!*

Afternoon's Impossible Heat

Afternoon's impossible heat;
I meditate; I need something
—boredom's illness
imprisons souls lost to idleness.

In half-awake daydreams:
I see spent memories, the future's death,
pieces of old clouds. My feelings
never rest.

For a long time
I've looked for existence.
I meditate; I need something;
my creative potency

is writing again: If suffering
is an art then what is happiness?

Upon My Lips

Upon my lips,
the salt of the sea;
the sand is my lover
(I have many earthly lovers)

—the roundness
of its bottom under my feet.

I awaken from a daydream
to find myself naked and
running like a sandpiper,

my lively genitals wet
from the breaking waves.

Blessed are the sun's rays
giving me life, sweat, desire,
sexual hunger and passion.

A young, raven-haired woman
is dancing in circles,
repeating the chakra mantras
(within each circle,

another piece of her clothing
floats to the water):
Her sexy nakedness

(like divinity fluffing her wings)
could heal the world.

She repeats herself:
Lam, Vam, Ram, Yam, Ham, Om
(earth, water, fire, air, space, eternity).

Her essence is spreading through the water:
I go to my knees
and drink from her joy.

Gratitude inflates my heart
as her eyes hold the horizon
—I must go there.

Moon, My Lover

Moon, my Lover—I have whispered this before
—staring at her warm stillness above a red evening;

clouds flee into crimson over the sea
—the sea honors moon, passing salt into the air.

Resting my heart against a sand dune, and
having mastered *stillness and silence,*

I am imprinting the waves with exhales
—rejuvenating my soul.

A full woman with dark nipples riding high
dances to her inner music.

Her joyful nakedness is blessed light.
Repeating her rhythmic motion,

the sea begins wetting her dark hairs
—beneath the water, her feet

drink the salt, algae, and sand.
Against the voicing sunset

her aura's radiance is brilliant.
The sea has discovered her belly button.

I face the joyful woman as if facing eternity; pleasurably,
my eyes depart hers, descending

to the promise of her luscious breasts.
Bowing to woman's pure-form,

I taste the air she dances in: Salt lingers in my mouth,
dissolves into my body.

Moon approaches a corner of the sky
dressed in pink clouds;

now,
moon burns yellow.

Harbin

It's the land, the harmonic energy coming from the land,
coupled with the natural scent of purity coming
from the spiritual essence of hot mineral water
fulfilling a promise to cleanse, not only the body
but the soul, too.

There are so many assortments of idyllic
peacefulness lingering in the air, one on top
of the other and side-by-side, making for an effortless
release of friction, or resistance, or any other kind of
dis-harmonic-stress-vibration.

The hypnotic circling of sun and moon, one sinking,
one rising, revolving, watching, all of the time under
a day-sky of sensual blue, or a night-sky of starry glimmer

—an unimaginable glimmer of dense fire against
space-black-evidence of eternity.

Some dawns rise warm and dry, other dawns rise
brisk and dewy; the air, permeated with earth's raw,
clean odor, is deliciously scented, alive, and pure.

It's the sound of voices whispering coupled with
the babbling brook's soothing water-tone-trance
of deep relaxation and Utopian calm while submerged
in the mother-like womb of hot mineral pools.

It's the way the light draws dreamy shadows of
heavenly nakedness against flowers blooming delicate
bouquets in vivid colors splashed with sun or moon light,
and the way the wild animals—the turkeys and the deer
—stroll, graze, and meander amongst the human energy,
coexisting in surreal harmony.

The *celestial-light atmosphere* creates a circulation of
expansive spiritual illumination cascading from the
tops of the surrounding mountains to the canyon that
swaddles the hot springs within a luscious forest of
trees, ferns, and floral bushes.

This enchanting experience conjures images of
the *Garden Of Eden* rising, breathing, and resuming
its joyful mythical energy of impossible love melodies,
of ethereal light, of *goddess* ecstasy, pure freedom,
and primitive easiness with slow, mystical ascensions
of love, comfort, affection, compassion,
respect, and pleasure.

Harbin Hot Springs
Lake County, California

Father, I Have Sinned

...then, there is their destiny as if a rotten
vein, as if Jesus, through his thorns, shed
their destiny for them with his loving blood.

Behind white walls, behind locked
white doors, the *White Whip* cracks its tip
and hate heats up its ferocious beast.

In this vision:
The warriors, those taught herds
of predators, fall to their knees
near the kill, and choking on
the pungent perfume of spilt blood,
scream up at the sky, "Father, I have sinned,
I have committed a mortal sin!"

Like imprisoned flocks, the warriors' spirits
suffer in their master's cage; confusion
touches one grave after another, and

the world, dressed in pain,
burns its deadly oil.

Commentary:

A large part of the U.S. Military is Christian.

Their 6th Holy Commandment states:

Thou Shall Not Kill (it does not list

any exceptions). To kill is a mortal sin

unforgivable by their *God*.

If I were to regret anything in my life

it would be having been drafted into

the U.S. Army from 1970 to 1972,

working as an artillery gunner for

the 3rd Infantry/39th Artillery.

Peace will never be attained through war.

May the Universal Spirit forgive us for this mistake.

If Only *God*

If only *God*
could breathe in then exhale
all of the corpses of love
back to life:

They would breathe again
within earth's pureness.
They would love again,
the air laced with their
blessed sound waves.

My heart wants love,
enough to cause
a whirlwind of oceans boiling,
enough to melt humanity's poisons
back to pure prairies, deserts,
horizons (rinsed in warm
joy)

—my dream, my soul, my longing.
God's flaws surround us:
This is not love!
Nursing my hunger for love's
delicate heart,

I live to drink the light from star clusters
(where the souls of the corpses of love
are put away):

I love their texture, their milky borders,
their white nights, their proper illumination

—I slump back into my soul,
waiting for *God* to exhale
all of the corpses of love
back to life.

Because *God* Is A Dream

There is promise in spiritual immortality, in the power of imagination,
and in the core belief of a disciplined futurist:

Imagine a future without *God*, or a future without ever saying the word
God. Perfection is imagination's desire, or its interest

in feeling perfect: Infinity is perfect. To breathe without *God* is perfection:
Nothing could be more perfect because *God* is a dream,

an inner image of psychic surrealism. The future believes in itself, in its
movements and currents, in the five physical realities, in its own light,

believes in its fundamental perfection of constant transformation, believes
in its own process of life and death:

Let us enter the future with no more guides or leaders for our spirits,
no more glorification of invisible deities; let us enter closer to ourselves.

Let us decline to contribute to the guild of men who excluded women
in the making of commandments for humanity: *Excluded women!*

The future is perfect because it leaves the past behind in its own nowhere:
If we don't say the word *God* then the *god-concept*

does not exist and existence still lives within its movements and currents
into the future, into perfection, into infinity.

They have named the universe *God*, and because of this name,
God has risen above us in a stream of *synthetic luminosity*;

let us see our bodies as light, as spiritual beings of transfigured form,
already enlightened—*already enlightened!*

—because we are the light
that we seek.

My Imagination

My imagination has launched
a thousand myths, centuries
of love, faces, death, songs,

invisible vessels of strange beauty,
of spirits and consciousness, of
inarticulate bruises and

tantalizing adjectives of disfigured
pronunciation expressing mystical
eroticism in all of its enigma:

I acknowledge the poetic order
of creation, the expanding sessions
of life and death, and the wide-spread
failure of human intelligence

in understanding the natural
healing force of multiple orgasms.

In the construction of my thoughts,
feelings, and actions, an undisciplined
hunger surges from my soul,
expressing an existential ambivalence

leading to
a transformational mystical eroticism
between two perfect opposites

—male/female, light/dark,
life/death, in/out, etc. etc.

—for only one purpose: *Bliss-Absolute.*

Beyond all other expressions, laws,
or fundamentalist dogma, only
mystical erotic bliss conveys

the true source of human longing.

And I honor universal eroticism
in all of its manifestations: *meteorites*
thrusting into planets, super novas,
plant sprouts pushing through earth's skin,
thermal water gushing from a
mountain, the bloody devouring of
a gazelle by a heated lion, a
man going down on a woman,
butterflies eating flowers,
flowers sucking air,
women giving birth, long slow
tantric positions.

All of these and more are
the true sonnets of life, of longing
for life, of tasting life

—nothing else matters:

not *God*, nor religion, nor hate,
nor nations, nor wars, nor money,
nor relationships, nor youth, nor jobs,
nor dreams,

nor, nor, nor... .

Boundless bliss surges from
erotic souls seeking the gratefulness
of other erotic souls seeking bliss:

There is no God greater than the God you are.

Gazing down at Wild Cat canyon delightfully dreamy
in dawn's delicate dew, there, light comes as if suddenly
a spirit separating its soul from the sun.

Light is a miraculous expression of life, beautifully
conceived with bright eyes for seeing in the dark and
persuasive fingers for coaxing shy flower buds to bloom,

and standing tall and erect in a body that has carried me
through seven-hundred-and-twenty full moons, plus
a dozen or more blue moons, I am vigorous and as
persistent as an alchemist persuading gold from lead.

My heart is endlessly young, a sacred love-fire
birthing light, a poem with its own voice, holding
sunbeams and moon-glow in its pulsing chambers
—and life dazzles me to no-end

because I have out-grown the melancholic emptiness,
the self-inflicted loneliness, and the insane suspicions
of my perplexed youth—now I am convinced that
That Wild Man Living In The Sky is neither

Father nor Shepard of my life, and that he is
emotionally absent and incapable of being
the sole creator of this phenomenal and
extraordinary universe, and
what am I to think of synthetic-religion's ability to

enclose the mind, or even worse, to stagnate the mind's
individual spiritual force?—what am I to think of this

when life is magic within magic, a grand illusion,
a cosmic crystal, a mystical pipe-line of souls seeking
physical sensations: sight, smell, sound, touch, and taste.
We are the magicians of our lives, the mystics, the wizards,
the shamans, and creators, the story-makers, story-tellers,
the editors and publishers:

I have created seven hundred and twenty full moons
in my life, a life that has been good and kind, bad
and unkind, a dance, a fall, a crawl; have been beaten
by a street gang, on my death bed once, have buried
my stoic father and manic mother, am a father to a daughter,
have lost loves only to find other loves, have tripped and
crashed emotionally only to get up and stand tall again,

and I refuse to point my finger at anybody and say:
This is your fault, all of the hardships in my life are
your fault—I refuse to say this to anybody.

I accept my fortunes and misfortunes as my creations
—how about you?

Thus-far, 720 full moons and now my hair is as
beautifully and majestically silver as each moon, and
there is a glowing grin on my mug as mischievous as
the Cheshire Cat's splendid smirk.

Between Happiness And Sadness

Between happiness and sadness
—silence;
an angel prays:

I kiss the loneliness of old people,
their temples like handfuls
of winter; their hearts

are used baggage, waiting;
memories speak to them,
they smile and

tell me stories from their youth
—sadness falls;
silence passes unspoken

—they remember the dead.
I kiss the loneliness
from their temples

and sadness lifts
from their mouths.

Now With My Youth Undone

Now with my youth undone,
I see only the beauty in aging:
myself, nothing but
a passing garment, or a slow cloud,
that the wind pushes against.

Somewhere, after my body surrenders
(to the cold, hard blood beneath
the darkness)
I will be in *stillness and silence*

—eyes empty; hands trusting;
my cold heart, now
the most eternal of all truth,
decaying near a sea weeping
foam and salt as my body's

skin and bones decompose
into death's dramatic scene.
In the open sky of my thoughts
(where surrealism manifests its reasons)

the desperate need to hold on
is obsolete, no longer voicing fear,
and what's left from my breath
will float away, like submissive bubbles

charged by the wind and rising,
into the air, into another light.

Then everything is forgotten,
like ocean swells breaking
into the sand and leaving
nothing left of the wave.

Then The Tumblers Rust

One day, which may come to exist, already
itself with thick shadows, I will sit near
the entrance where light becomes morning.

Rising dawn, its shape like a prayer in the
hands of existence, never deceiving itself
nor those who assemble like pure clouds,
is sure to be nothing more than
invisible ether flooding creation.

It's as simple as this: That which glitters
in dreams or in life's last footprint
is understood as *Spiritual Essence*.

Nothing but heaven with its living mirror
reflects who we are: the light, love, tears,
the stones, dust, minerals, the changing tides,
the one magnetic way.

Between now and then the pleasantness of breathing,
its cool moisture, motion, divine invasion, and
truthful comfort, will find its way without feathers
or song, will find its tomorrow with a different key
for unlocking another dimension:

Light darkens, wings carry seeds, kisses leave
no lasting smears, and death's integrity is a gift.

As always, the old way and the new way forever
revolve and never really change: Still, the *Toll Keeper*
collects the tickets (the hopes, visions, and opinions)
just before departure calls out and carries our spirits
to the *Light House* whose beacon, over time, fades
into stillness, silence, and disbelief.

Most of the time I listen to the trees breathing,
to the salty breath of breaking waves, and to leftover souls
in deep mirrors begging to be cracked. I listen to
the bladed edge of words that stop just before
cutting into thin-skinned emotions.

I have talked with the balancing point of *Life's Harmony*,
with the distance *Forever* promises, with *Memories*
that have no choice but to remember.
I have talked with *Wisdom*, which told me:

Another time. Another time.

Soon it will be night and I will sit at the portal
where light leaves, to see it off on its own
living journey, to its destination of another dimension,

to where the dead turn the lock with their keys:
It opens, they enter, and it locks again.
Then the tumblers rust.

What Have I Learned?

What have I learned?
With longing, I carry my life in my heart:
A flock of songbirds, estranged friends, a
child (a young girl), happiness, unhappiness

—inside my heart is a train station; a soul
walking, not walking; a long platform;
understood loneliness; blank destinations;
routine days; the happiness of soft collisions.

My heart—a suitcase I have filled and emptied,
filled and emptied (so many times)
until I have opened my chest screaming:

The spineless skeletons of estranged friends litter the tracks!

Steam from my heart forms a sizeable cloud, a distant youth,
dreams that have never come true—have I grown frightened?

I have dug my fingernails into the air, digging
for descriptive sounds: verbs, nouns, adjectives. Love! Love!
The ocean at my doorstep: Love!
The ocean: my lover, my blood, and soul
—it's through you life on earth sustains.

How many times have I daydreamed out loud:
Listen! Listen to the sea (*Neruda*: my brother!).

Listen to *The Captain's Verses*,
or the evening's hands clapping with stars: Love! Love!

The wind's clarity passes over my breath: I breathe! I breathe!
Returning to the source, I see tracks across the sky, footprints.

Once, *Jesus* walked through the air, suitcase in hand, saying:
I can't do anything more for you people! He evaporated.
They watched him and, still,
love has no phone number, no hot line.

What have I learned?

At The End Of Each Day

At the end of each day I go over my visions,
fantasies, and daydreams

—to see which ones have materialized.
I recharge my mind with primal energy.

Between evening
and dawn the stars unravel;

I walk barefoot in *Garden Luscious*
and night moths quiet themselves;

night birds split their songs
on blades of sharp leaves.

I press my thoughts against breath and
enter my silence through memories:

Down, somewhere, near the beginning of my past,
joy lost its shape (more than once).

Too many times I fell backwards,
spiraling and, for a while, when

I would see anything spiraling
toward me, I'd unfold like a bad sentence

while muttering to myself,
asking that light never leave me.

Now, I am the light, the vision, the fantasy,
the living daydream, the *god* I have been seeking:

There is no God greater than the God you are.

About the Author

Born in Herkimer, New York, in 1950, and raised in Ilion, New York, Dah has been writing poetry since 1961 and has penned nearly five-thousand works of poetry and prose, sometimes writing up to ten pieces a day. Although his work has been published in anthologies and on literary websites, *In Forbidden Language* is his first full-length collection.

He is currently working on his second book of poetry as well as work including poems and some of his award-winning photography. Dah has lived in Berkeley, California since 1980 and, for the past ten years, has been teaching Chakra Four Yoga® and Meditation to children and adults.

I envy (in a manner of speaking) any man who has the time to prepare something like a book and who, having reached the end, finds the means to be interested in its fate or in the fate which, after all, it creates for him.

André Breton, 1928

www.ingramcontent.com/pod-product-compliance
Lightning Source LLC
Chambersburg PA
CBHW031849090426
42741CB00005B/420